The Grass Is the First to Go

10 plays to stimulate and elucidate our thinking about how we live and treat each other

ORLANDO CEASER

The Grass Is the First to Go

Published by Watchwell Communications, Inc. Offices in South Barrington, IL and Chicago, IL.

ISBN: 978-0-9907555-9-3- Paperback
ISBN: 978-0-9907555-0-0 E-book

Cover Design: Rachael Proulx

Library of Congress Cataloging – in – Publication Data:
Ceaser, Orlando

For more information, please contact:
Orlando.ceaser@watchwellinc.com
Tele: 847-812-5006 (mobile)

Mailing Address:
Watchwell Communications, Inc.
P.O. Box 3783
Barrington, Illinois 60011
847-812-5006
224-848-4074 (fax)

www.OrlandoCeaser.com,
www.ozoneleadership.com,
www.watchwellinc.com,
www.teachthechildrentodance.com,
www.myozonelayer.com

Printed in the United States of America

I dedicate this book to the life and legacy of my Father, Norrell Ceaser, Sr., and his loving wife Ruby Lenora Ceaser. They had 11 children, 29 grandchildren and 13 great grandchildren. My parents are in my DNA, my heart and my memories. Their legacy will live on through generations.

Also by Orlando Ceaser

Books

- *Daily Resurrections*
- *FREE*
- *I Wake-up Wanting You*
- *Leadership above the Rim -The Poetry of Possibility*
- *Leadership Greatness through High Performance Poetry*
- *Look for the Blessing*
- *Teach the Children to Dance*
- *The Isle of Knowledge*
- *Unlock the Secrets of Ozone Leadership*
- *Unlock Your Leadership Greatness*
- *Unlock Your Leadership Greatness – For Students*

CDs

- *Leadership Collection*
- *My Queen*
- *Teach the Children to Dance*

Comic Strips

- *Cocky and Rhodette*
- *Cocky Jr.*
- *Π Rats*

Website addresses:

- www.OrlandoCeaser.com,
- www.watchwellinc.com
- www.OzoneLeadership.com
- www.teachthechildrentodance.com
- The “O” Zone Blog: www.myozonelayer.com

ACKNOWLEDGEMENTS

I pay homage to the change agents who consistently apply their mission to improve the plight of millions of people around the world; people and organizations who commit their time and resources to change the world through positive efforts that make a difference.

I owe people who stand up against, and resist, the forces that try to break them and make them assimilate and suppress their gifts. I applaud the students and young adults who, recognizing the sacrifices of their ancestors, answer the call and commitment of their faith to do good and to do better. Young people strive to hold us accountable in the face of hypocritical actions. There are individuals like Shaundra Ceaser, my niece, who volunteers and takes steps to change the world, beginning with her local community. She is active and speaks out against oppression and injustice.

There are countless parents who accept the challenges and the charge to guide the footsteps of their offspring in the direction of success and survival. I see them as I speak at parent meetings in elementary and high schools around Chicago. Often, their children struggle against the pressure from their peers to hide their gifts and conform to behavior which goes against their upbringing. I remember the same feelings as a child. I acknowledge and thank these parents and other adults who intervene to help them feel safe and give these children and young adults the foundation, environment and values to resist mediocrity and actions that will send them down unproductive paths. Additionally, I acknowledge the adults who line the safe passage routes throughout Chicago's neighborhoods to ensure that children can travel safely to and from school.

I applaud non-profits, businesses and other organizations that are committed to helping the greater communities of which they are a part. They demonstrate this commitment by dedicating financial resources and the time and energy of their people to feed the hungry, provide shelter and address violence. Organizations such as the Black Star Project and its founder, Phillip Jackson, are actively engaged in "Peace in the Hood" initiatives and other activities on the frontline to assist in the struggles of the disenfranchised in Chicago and beyond.

I thank Nicole Ceaser, my niece, for an amazing picture of me and my Dad that is on the last page of this book.

I thank churches like Willow Creek Community Church, in South Barrington, Illinois and Senior Pastor, Bill Hybels who educate and inspire their membership to assist the poor and marginalized, as instructed by Jesus Christ. Pastor Hybels is committed to his church following Jesus and reflecting the diversity of Heaven. Daily, his congregations, through God-inspired servants such as Steve Carter, Scott Pederson, Heather Larsen and Anne Rand, have a profound effect upon people around the world. In addition to its many impressive outreach efforts, Willow Creek has an active Prison and Jail Ministry that makes regular visits to the incarcerated and last year the Church created care packages for every incarcerated person in Illinois, which exceeded 50,000 people.

I shall be forever grateful to my parents, Norrell and Ruby Ceaser, who have always stimulated my thinking and encouraged me to spread the messages of peace, justice, leadership and love.

PREFACE

Poets are practitioners of the art of observation. We chronicle the world around us and, through inspired interpretation, record events for posterity. We seek clarity, as we strive to understand life. Poets may be preachers or prophets or simply the silent people with opinions. If solicited, we could acknowledge reality and notify others about our commonality, so that our differences can be used to fortify a strong bond. Our similarities and differences can bring us together.

The *Grass Is the First to Go* is a set of one-act plays, created in reaction to life and its prevailing social issues. I intended these plays to be performed in classrooms, prisons, businesses and houses of worship. I performed similar plays in a verse choir at Antioch Baptist Church in Cleveland, Ohio. Theater has emerged as a powerful medium of expression and talent development in prisons and jails. As such, I envision these one-act plays as source material for the incarcerated. These issues described herein, cry out to be noticed, debated and altered, where necessary. It is my hope that these plays well spark deeper conversations and greater understanding among people who are different.

My views for this book were shaped by numerous relocations as a part of my career advancement, conversations with my wife, children, teammates, managers, mentors and many others. My observations were accumulated over decades of raising children, walking and working in the presence of diverse populations and managing within a corporate environment.

I have seen the rise and demise of neighborhoods and relationships. I have seen anger in the streets and department stores. I have watched the poor and others protest. I have also witnessed people wrap themselves in their own opinions and worldview. I have heard people question their personal interests and why they focus on transient points of insignificance while the world grapples with greater problems.

The *Grass Is the First to Go* began as poetic observations that were stylized accounts of personal observations and experiences. These poems eventually took on multiple voices to capture and communicate the challenges faced within the human race. Ultimately, the poems grew in scope and length, as they told me, they were incomplete. They voice their intention to be controversial, provocative and transformative. They demand to be spoken by different voices, to become plays of possibility with scenes of significance, to address and amplify some of the key challenges of today.

Some of the observations and interpretations are challenging and explosive. My intent is to remove the bandage quickly from the wounds of life. The wounds should be exposed to the healing atmosphere of an open mind.

The *Grass Is the First to Go* gives language and vocabulary to audiences who are not well informed about people who are different from them. "Affirmations in Incarceration" and "The Prisoners Pledge" both reflect on presentations and conversations with those who were housed in our nation's penal system. I spoke to inmates at the Metropolitan Correctional Center at their GED graduation ceremony in Chicago. I spoke to prisoners who presented to members at the Willow Creek Community Church Prison and Jail Ministry. Additionally, I have had conversations with individuals in law enforcement and those who spoke through the Black Star Project to Chicago public school children about prisons and jails.

"A Stranger: The Legend of a Random Black Guy" draws from the fact that in our culture, there is a specter of negativity surrounding the African-American male. Too many crimes are committed and the description is that of an African-American male, whether they did it or not. I was stopped by two police officers while in high school. I was placed against the car and frisked. I asked the police officers what was the problem? They stated that an African-American male fitting my description stole a lady's purse at 79th and Euclid Avenue. I informed the officers that I was actually running toward 79th and Euclid Avenue. Therefore, I felt they were stopping any random Black guy on the street.

"Am I Black Enough?"addresses a struggle and dialogue among people who left neighborhoods, never lived in the neighborhood and those who reside in and never left the neighborhood. The tension exists between those who did not wish to conform to certain practices, behaviors and expectations. These individuals were made to feel substandard, inauthentic and counterfeit. There were sent on a guilt trip and deemed unworthy to wear the mantle of Blackness. "Am I Black enough?" faces this issue head-on with a compelling conversation.

"Alien Nate and Me" stages an interaction with an extraterrestrial who questions man's inhumane treatment of its fellow man, as he seeks to explore and understand the rationale behind our thinking and actions.

"I Protest" makes statement that there are many forms of protest. People march, sit in or boycott companies or products. Some will protest by obstruction and others by destruction. The poetic voice seeks to bring the various forms of disobedience out into the open, to be understood. Nonviolent protest against injustice should always have a place in our discourse. When our young people speak out against inequality and injustice, we must understand their discomfort, because we have raised them to be intolerant of these practices.

"Meaningful Messages" is a piece that calls out to individuals who may play a role in the perpetuation of violence in inner cities around the world and implores them to stop the violence.

"My Life Defined" speaks to our propensity to concentrate on aspects of life that are menial, meaningful and meaningless. Where are we? Do we reach out to commune and break bread with those who are different, as well as those who are similar?

"Old Players Home for Broken Down Lovers" I watched as young men celebrate the mindset of being a player. These individuals are described as being cool and very lucky with the ladies. Players don't want to be tied down and they may have several children out of wedlock with different mothers. Their freewheeling lifestyle invariably takes a toll on the emotions and economics of people in the neighborhood.

"The Grass Is the First to Go" is the signature play in this collaboration. It was inspired by childhood observations. I was aware of people who moved into beautiful neighborhoods, which ultimately were diminished by lack of care. They had beautiful lawns and greenery which highlighted the streets. I watched the children play and noticed there were no boundaries, as they raced across the lawns, with no concern for the grass. Years later, when I returned to these areas, I noticed the grass was run down or eliminated. The same lack of discipline on the lawns showed up in other areas. The homes and apartments, attitudes and behavior had that same rundown lack of discipline approach reflected in the absence of the well manicured lawns.

The Grass Is the First to Go challenges our thinking. There is value in authentic and accurate reporting, but the interpretation is in the mind of the thinker. The periodic cry of "keeping it real" should not negate the heart's desire to reach for what is possible. We should not lock ourselves behind barriers that shield us from reality. Additionally, we should not sink to lower levels, as one trapped in the quicksand of regression, negativity and lack of growth.

These 10 one-act plays are for your reading enjoyment and utilization. You are only limited by your imagination, as to how and where these works may be staged and presented. Your ultimate goal should be to spark a flame conversation about our current reality and the necessity to change to improve the human condition.

The Grass Is the First to Go provides inspiration for conversations on its content, in an effort to convert content into communications and change communications into connection and correction.

CONTENTS

A STRANGER: THE LEGEND OF A RANDOM BLACK GUY

by
Orlando Ceaser

"A STRANGER: THE LEGEND OF A RANDOM BLACK GUY"

Fade In:

Narrator
He is the anti-superhero,
The Devil's deadly spawn;
Who strikes at nightfall
Or just before dawn.

His legend is mythical;
His movements are cyclical;
With power and the presence to appear
When they least expect him,
They will detect him
In their minds he is their greatest fear.

Reader 1
They see him at the end of the bar
Mysteriously sitting alone.
He seems to show up wherever they are.
You cannot trust him
He may follow you home.

He is seen walking along the highway
Without a container for gasoline;
As people drive by
They release a sigh
And wonder if he'll cause a scene.

Reader 2

They claim he was loitering on busy streets.
Whenever he's present a threat exists.
He seems suspicious, reluctant to meet.
He stares in their faces, they clench their fists.

He is frequently in the department stores
Perusing the inventory.
They have the feeling they've seen him before,
On breaking news, as a feature story?

Reader 3

A stranger, a random black guy on display;
He's poised and prepared to ruin their day.
Some residents are intimidated.
Some want him extinct, eliminated.

Folks deny evidence that won't support
Their claim that he should be in jail or court,
Awaiting a sentence
For some atrocity,
More substantive than curiosity.
Some claim he's the culprit behind all ills;
Society's wrongs are also his fault.
He's unemployed, lazy but has the skills,
To damage property with each assault.

Reader 4

Grab your purses for he is on the prowl;
Protect your children, hide your womenfolk.
He is on the move with motives so foul,
Financially weak and morally broke.

He is a criminal, he must be framed;
Mr. Anonymous, unknown, unnamed.
He is genetically predisposed to lie.
He is a stranger,
A random black guy.

Reader 1
Outraged citizens shout obscenities;
When he's present in their vicinity.
He's mentally charged and presumed guilty.
He can't be on the streets and be guilt free.
If police encounter an angry mob,
They would find deputies to do their jobs.

The sketch artist draws a depiction
Of his face from the witnesses conviction,
Not their memory in hopes that later
A random black guy, the perpetrator
Will be shamelessly apprehended
And given the sentence recommended.

Reader 3
He is the convenient statistic;
An angry young man that goes ballistic.
Sane people say they are about to die
When they see a stranger,
A random black guy.

He is a drain on the economy,
He is there, even if not seen.
He is a strain and his autonomy
Supports a bevy of welfare queens.

Reader 2
He is causing the nation to falter.
They subsidize the time he spends in jail.
He will cause them to waver and alter;
Unless justice finds a way to prevail.
His influence and power enlarges,
Until put away on trumped up charges.

He gets the blame for the most heinous acts,
When victims are seen on the evening news;
Implicated in malicious attacks,
The subject of countless interviews.

Reader 4
At the scene of the crime, police rely
On eye witness testimonies to find,
The face of a stranger, a random black guy,
Who is embedded deep within their minds.

He is ubiquitous and gets around,
In gated communities some retreat.
They move to the countryside, but he is found
Whenever violence occurs in the streets.

Reader 1
He cannot be rehabilitated,
Because the cures won't last.
He is always a suspect, related
To the sins of the past.

He is among the usual suspects,
Who are corralled out of the clear blue sky;

It is a valid reason to select,
A profile to match a random black guy.

Reader 4
The sober tale of a random black guy;
A legend farfetched, a villain supreme;
A composite sketch that some won't deny;
A nightmare to haunt your dreams.

Man has a tendency to walk in fear;
And is haunted by what he can't forgive;
We see a villain when someone appears
In different places from where they live;
They recognize that he is out of place;
A terror to citizens of each race?

Reader 3
Some need guns and second amendment rights,
Or they think they will wake up to the sound
Of a burglar walking some hot summer night,
Into their bedroom and snooping around.

Reader 2
And they will send him to meet his maker
Insisting he was the perpetrator.'
In a pine box from the undertaker
They will send him back to his Creator;
Even with an iron clad alibi,
They may rush to judgment to see him die.

Fade Out:

THE END

AFFIRMATIONS IN INCARCERATION

by
Orlando Ceaser

"AFFIRMATIONS IN INCARCERATION"

Fade In:

Reader 1
I will,
Seize opportunities to advance
My position to keep dreams alive;
Use time as a resource to enhance,
And strive and survive and thrive.

Reader 2
I was not born, so others could die,
My greatest appeal is not to steal;
There is a power greater than I,
That's working on the anger I feel.

Reader 3
My children suffer when I am jailed;
Testosterone raging in my bones,
Makes me tough as nails, but I have failed,
If my children are at home alone.

Reader 4
I can't be a father behind bars,
The kind of father I know they need.
I'm role modeling tattoos and scars,
They want changes to the life I lead.

Reader 5
They are my responsibility.
I am in here for my infractions.
I am housed in this facility;
Held accountable for my actions.

Reader 6
I give permission in my new role
To let go of my need to control,
As I surrender and show remorse,
I seek forgiveness, my life's on course.

Reader 1
I need to throw anger overboard
And submit my temper to my Lord;
Approach the Father, Son and Holy Ghost,
To be my advocate and my coach.

Reader 2
My dysfunctional family tree;
The negative nature in the streets;
Being paralyzed by poverty;
Underserved makes it hard to compete.

Reader 3
There's insufficient education;
Associating with the wrong crowd;
Drugs and alcohol were temptation;
In the gang family I am proud.

Reader 4
A father figure is on vacation;
Not around to show me the ropes.
Looking for love and validation;
Somewhere along the way, losing hope.

Reader 5
So my record makes it hard for me;
To get a job and live with my kids.
I want the dream of my legacy,
To not be held back for what I did.

Reader 6
I feel the world is out to get me;
Society has this evil plan;
A conspiracy that won't let me,
Remove barriers, work like a man.

Reader 1
To the best of my ability;
I will harness my hostility;
For my rehabilitation,
Will lead to reconciliation.

Reader 2
My change in heart is evident,
As my consent reveals my intent,
My life expectancy should increase;
I want to live 'til I rest in peace.

Reader 3
I will seek the life for which I've dreamed;
I know through faith I have been redeemed.
I know that life will be difficult,
But I will work for a good result.

Reader 4
I ask forgiveness of those I've hurt,
Those I've despised and treated like dirt.
I hope the harmed and disappointed,
One day think I've been anointed.

Reader 5
I know I will be tempted to blame
Society and authority,
For all the suffering and the shame,
That made revenge my priority.

Reader 6
Incarceration has restrictions,
And challenges which may complicate
My life, but I won't let convictions
Become a prediction of my fate.

Fade Out:

THE END

ALIEN NATE AND ME

by
Orlando Ceaser

"ALIEN NATE AND ME"

Fade In:

Me

I met an alien, his name was Nate,
It is short for Nathan, Nathaniel
The Great.
We could relate
On many issues,
We could contrast and compare.
We were so different,
But eager to share.

I met him one night during
A lightning storm.
The temperature in my room,
Tepid, warm.
I saw this figure slowly transform;
A whirling dervish
Swirling in a swarm of energy
That slowly converted to look like me.

Nate

He told me honestly
How he was surprised,
By my normal shaped head
And regular eyes.
I asked why he labeled me
Insidious
And I asked why the unknown
Is always hideous.

Me
I met an alien his name was Nate,
I dealt delicately with his confusion.
He could not understand man's rate
Of arrogance and exclusion.
He said that we were granted dominion
Over the animals and the elements,
Yet, we performed in his opinion
In ways illogical and irrelevant.

He was inquisitive
And picked my brain,
For reasons that could contain
The roots of logic,
To examine what he sees;
To justify the behavior of my species;
Obsessed with the will to win;
Soaked in selfishness,
Programmed to sin.

I met an alien his name was Nate,
I asked him to be clear and elaborate,
On the planet he left to visit mine,
To learn about his culture and refine
My understanding, so I could immerse
Myself in knowledge of his universe.

Nate
We are united with similar goals.
We have our differences in actions and roles,
But we are not competitive,
Striving to be superior;

Beauty and love are on the interior
And exterior,
Without the need to make
Others inferior.

I can elaborate about the atmosphere.
We take care of our planet
And our work and careers.
We are focused on loving one another.
It is not merely a logo or slogan.
Once our civilization was broken,
Then we arrived at a point
Of being outspoken
About love being our salvation,
So we became open
To our sisters and brothers,
And working together to
Thrive more than survive,
Enjoying life and grateful
To be alive.

Me
I met an alien, his name was Nate,
Who wondered why we discriminate.

Nate
Why do human beings with similar stories
Place each other in categories?
And why do you differentiate
And through differences
Fail to communicate.

Why wouldn't you work as a union,
For the improvement of all mankind,
Or engage in sweet communion,
Respectful of each other's hearts and minds.
Why do you shun equality
Where some have to be on top
And some below?
Why is it difficult to give an apology
When guided by the id and ego.

How can you sleep when refugees are displaced;
Nations are plundered and disgraced?
Why are you personally locked on greed;
Ferociously protecting selfish needs
And reckless with animosity;
Dismissing love and generosity.

Me
He wondered why we pillaged and plundered
And raped the residents of the villages under
Our judgment and jurisdiction;
Why we conquer with conviction
And savagely dismember our own
With brutality that animals have seldom shown.

Nate
How can so many people ever come together,
Unless you had to face invaders from science fiction?
Must a catastrophe reveal common convictions,
To successfully navigate and avoid
Attacks from pestilence or asteroids?
You must unite around a common threat.

Must you fear total annihilation,
Before you address
Violations against a universal moral code
And barbarous acts and heinous crimes
Perpetrated in these scandalous
And perilous times?

Me
I met an alien, his name was Nate
Selfishness he felt was
An inefficient use of resources;
A waste of potential and energy.
It did not maximize the forces
That existed, the synergy,
Inherent within our legacy.
Speak to us about your success,
Eliminating hopeless and bitterness.

Nate
We banished hopelessness and bitterness.
They vanished when dreams were subsidized.
We would not let people consider less
Than their potential fully utilized.
We do not have sex trafficking or genocide,
Nor a slave trade or exploitation, pride
Is practical to cause and we abstain
From harming others for personal gain;
A fanatical focus on pleasure,
Is illogical, but we treasure life.

We have found purpose and do not rush
To the end of the day,
Crushing competitors along the way,

We do not disrespect with incivility,
Armed conflict and hostility.
When people challenge their institutions,
We don't let them dismantle and destroy.
They look inwardly for solutions,
They look inwardly for morality
And character to build their personalities.'

Me
I met an alien, his name was Nate,
He wanted to learn why people hate.
We discussed the universal fears;
Death, the outsider, insignificance,
The future and chaos, the difference
Between the occupants of our space;
Insecurities in the human race.

Nate
I would think you'd want to
Advance the species and protect
The Earth,
When children are born,
From the time of their birth,
They should be protected
And given a chance to prosper despite,
Arbitrary systems of wrong and right.

Me

He questioned our objectives,
When we were conditioned to be;
When we were zealots to our perspectives
The preoccupation with pleasure;
To supplant purpose, as its substitute
And the destruction of authority
And hammering our institutions
When they provide structure
And temporary solutions;
To the complexities of our existence,
Giving us the faith for persistence
And resistance.

I met an alien, his name was Nate
He wondered why we chose to complicate
Relationships with insincerity
And live our lives without clarity;
When we could establish expectations,
To remove guess work and speculation.
He felt we human were precarious
With insecurities that were nefarious.

Nate

Why do you visualize the world
And unknown sections of the universe,
As frightening regions under a curse?
Why do you see yourselves as the superior race,
When technologically your advances
May be common place.
You may need your confidence restored,

For your progress maybe mediocre at best
Among civilizations unexplored.

Me
I met an alien, his name was Nate,
It is short for Nathan, Nathaniel
The Great;
An extra-terrestrial born and raised,
In a galaxy where they never aged.

Nate
My people learned lessons
By following instructions
That were gifts from our leaders
Of conscious deduction;
To steer away from actions
That lead to destruction,
For many things make common sense;
To love one another
And come to the defense
Of anyone for we all are neighbors,
Created by God to learn from our labors;
And granted with gifts
To nourish and enhance
Our species in order to advance.

Me
I met an alien, his name was Nate,
He traveled the world to penetrate
Man's secrets and fear of the unknown;
His ego and propensity

To enslave his own;
His savage streak and need to rule,
His thirst for power and to ridicule.

Nate
I sat in silence, as he tried to explain.
Why human's nature causes so much pain.
We had a conversation about fate.
I would not confirm or deny,
Her belief in a deity beyond the sky.
I take solace, as a humble visitor,
From my cosmological celestial shore.

Me
Was he an angel from the other side?
Was he a messenger,
A fugitive on the run,
Searching for a place to hide?
Or was he my imaginary rabbit,
Like Harvey in the movies long ago?
My new friend challenged my habits,
Tried to make sense of my world,
Which also helped me to grow.

I met an alien,
His name was Nate,
He asked me to contemplate
And concentrate
On poverty and starvation;
Distribution of wealth
And property,
Among disparate nations;

And man's inhumanity to man;
The reality in our galaxy
That selfishness is a fallacy,
As a solution.
In God's plan,
Love is the answer,
Only love can address our ills
And give us peace
And the necessary skills
To live in harmony.

Fade Out:

THE END

AM I BLACK ENOUGH?

by
Orlando Ceaser

AM I BLACK ENOUGH?

Fade In:

Youth 1
Who do you think you are,
A bourgeois superstar?
You are fighting to let go
Living in the same ghetto,
But, you don't seem to know
Your place;
You think you're better
Than your race,
I don't think you're black enough.

Youth 2
You don't want to stay with us;
Think you're too good to play with us;
Don't want to spend another day with us.
If you could you would do away with us.
I think that if you could rewrite
History than you would be white,
For you seem to be so inclined,
To see the world as colorblind,
I don't think you're black enough.

Youth 3
You did not grow up in the hood,
Inner city life, you don't think is good;
In the suburbs living out near the woods;
Our way of life is misunderstood,

I bet you feel ashamed
When news comes on and we are blamed.
You want to disassociate from us,
With low self esteem and self hate
You try to keep it real,
But, you don't know how that feels.
I don't think you're black enough?

Youth 4
You are light, bright and damn near white;
A shallow variation of the night;
Leaning toward the brighter scale;
Rocking that lighter shade of pale.
How could you of the transparent hue;
Possibly know what I'm going through.
I'm dark in the hood where life is tough.
I don't think you are Black enough.

Narrator
The person who works hard and perseveres,
Hears voices activated by the fears
Of people who ask, Are you Black enough?
Do you find you're under attack enough?
Growing up did you watch your back enough,
As you fought each day of the week?
But, some folk display the mendacity,
To challenge you with audacity,
Discrediting your capacity,
To be authentic whenever you speak.

There are people who want others confined,
To an image that is found in their minds.

They will challenge them on their racial pride;
Call them names, intimidate until they reside
In turmoil from the relentless assault;
They have convinced themselves that it is their fault,

Student 1
They doubt my life was hard enough;
Was not hassled in the yard enough;
Walked the streets not on guard enough;
To identify with their pain.
They question time spent on the streets;
The hard knocks that took me off my feet;
Somehow they surmised my life as too sweet,
Therefore, I should not complain.

Student 2
Life was a gamble, a roll of the dice;
Put me in a place with no sacrifice
They feel I did not suffer, pay a price,
So they threaten to damage my esteem?
They have a certain image in mind;
I cannot be color blind,
If I'm a member of the team.
They think I am unusual
And must beg for acceptance and approval.

Student 3
I can tell you that your questions;
Fills my heart with indigestion.
I have a small suggestion,
That I feel you must pursue.

A lineage of Kings and Queens;
With excellence within our genes;
Great thinkers that history has seen,
So, I may ask how Black are you?

Student 4
How are you measuring the goal?
What standards are on your controls?
Are you playing positive roles?
That would make our ancestors proud.
We should consider it a crying shame
To torment people by playing games?
By degrading and calling names,
Intimidation is not allowed.

Student 2
For the record, I'm not speaking white,
I am speaking right,
The way the language is to be spoken;
I am growing skills in the open;
Trying to improve myself,
To improve my race;
Allow me to keep pace,
And enjoy the chase.
I'm writing a script you should not edit;
Why do you give white folks all the credit?
It is an issue that must be resolved.
Excellence and greatness cannot be dissolved.

Student 1
Did I keep it real in his reality?
Did I show in my personality?
Don't be threatened by the totality
Of a disciplined ambition.
Do you want me to feel guilty
And caught off guard,
But we both know that
Life is hard.
But, I don't need
To walk the same boulevard,
To understand your position.

Student 4
Insult me, you're insulting us;
During times that are tumultuous.
We must act adults to us,
Instead of traitors to the race.
You feel you had the right to facilitate
A conversation to humiliate,
An insurrection to debilitate.
Berate my character to my face.

Student 3
Who made you the standard bearer,
By which others are measured?
Why should I listen to you when
Your intentions are wrong,
You want me weak,
So you can appear strong.

Am I human enough, respect elders,
Stand as a strong role model to the tribe?
Are neighborhoods and villages the shelters,
The fortresses the ancestors described
And sang about in songs, so long ago,
Instructing us while walking to and fro,
To always hold our heads up with pride,
To be royal, loyal and dignified.

Narrator
Where is the diversity of thought?
Are we all supposed to think the same?
Where are values ancestors taught?
Where is the pride in the family name?
Let us be strong not to be corralled,
By group paranoia and rationale;
Let us avoid skin color debates,
Internal bickering that leads to hate.

Youth 1
I am no longer playing the
"Are you Black enough game?"
If you are trying to make it
I have no right to blame
You for trying to elevate your
Station in life,
By speaking properly,
Striving for prosperity,
Trying to build a business,
Obtain property,
Especially, when upward

Is the direction
You choose to move.
I salute you
And when you reach your goal,
We will all improve.

Student 1
I question the motives,
Of people who claim
To be on my side.
Yet, try to tear me down
And only provide
Barriers to block my way,
Carriers of negativity
To ruin my day.

Why taunt with meaningless definitions
And label me as the opposition.
Survivors guilt, do not hang that on me;
I want to live a life that is gang free.
The deteriorating neighborhood
Was sapping my hope and vitality
And punishing me, but I withstood
Discomfort for a new reality.

Student 2
Don't lift yourself
By trying to hold me down.
I need to climb higher to
Reach my crown
And if I differ in my
Point of view,

Don't condemn me
Because I don't think like you.

Student 3
Don't attack my family structure;
No one's perfect;
Dysfunction can rupture
The relationships, we should pursue
Or the ones we should renew.
I may have it lesser or better than you.
I may seem more together than you,
But don't let manufactured sin,
Block our progress before we begin.

Student 4
Did you stab me in the back enough?
Say I don't pick up the slack enough
Don't question if I'm black enough?
Help each other, so we proceed,
On a path where there is unity,
For the sake of the community,
God will grant us immunity,
To give each other what we need.

You will not make me guilty as before.
I will not feel inadequate anymore.
I will live life and relish the chance
I want to rise, react and advance.

Narrator
I've watched too many young boys and girls
With burdens of guilt and low self esteem,

They find themselves trapped between two worlds.
They try to excel and reach for their dreams;
Exercising talents from the Creator,
But, are made to feel like they're a traitor.
There's guilt and anguish striving for the crown,
To hold them back, people will hold them down.

Release families trying to get out,
Do not criticize them when they return,
Don't make them feel guilty, make them feel doubt;
Their education is their path to earn.
Give them your blessing as an endorsement;
So they view their support as reinforcement.

Welcome them and make them feel safe.
View their departure, not as an escape,
But a field trip to solve the mystery,
Of the greatness in our history,
And though the road traveled is difficult,
To hurt each other gives a bad result,
Because we need the means to inspire,
Everyone to aim and climb higher.

Fade Out:

THE END

I PROTEST

by
Orlando Ceaser

"I PROTEST"

Fade In:

Several readers are positioned on stage or on location on the streets facing the audience or the camera. They are serious in their demeanor, but determined in their delivery. The Narrator and at least 4 Readers are in the cast.

Narrator
Protest occurred and is documented at many places in human history. Change happened because a group or an individual decided they were not pleased and would no longer tolerate certain circumstances, governments, systems, practices or people. Expressing displeasure and discontent was through different means. Some were verbal or written. There were physical displays such as marches, strikes, sit-ins, boycotts and strikes.

Protest was also demonstrated through resistance of many kinds, passive aggressive behavior, obstructionism, lack of engagement and withholding productivity. Protests can be collective and personal, as people revolt and challenge the status quo for many reasons.

Protester 1
I protest to release my frustrations;
To force a change in a situation;
To shift the tone of the conversation
To negligence and discrimination;
Where the unfair practices can be cited

And tensions flared and passions ignited;
And meaningful talk across a wide range
Of issues necessary to bring change.

Protester 2
I protest to voice my displeasure;
Shout my discontent, so I can measure
Progress and wonder why it takes so long
To change a system we agree is wrong.
The extent of my dissatisfaction
Is evident in my angry reaction
To the continuous lack of respect
And willful periods filled with neglect.

Protester 3
I protest to achieve a specific goal;
To acquire some semblance of control;
By any means necessary change the score;
I'm mad as Hell and won't take anymore.
I can no longer take the senseless fights.
We must exercise our human rights,
For we must pursue and reach common ground,
Where dignity in progress can be found.

Protester 4
I protest even when they mock my voice
And misrepresent motives for my choice.
But, citizens rally to my defense
And challenge me when I'm not making sense;
For I rebel resisting the forces
That try to diminish the resources

And will not listen to valid concerns.
They say "Suffer in silence, wait your turn."

Protester 1
I strive through civil disobedience.
I sit. I march. I boycott or I pray.
My protest's a call for expedience;
I chant, when barriers are in my way.
I stand for justice without concessions;
My protest's a means of self expression.
And we should not need a revolution,
To arbitrate the proper solution.

Protester 2
Some think I protest just because I can,
But I have a reason, I have a plan
And an objective, a list of demands;
An open mind that tries to understand
That it may require a negotiation,
Where each side moves from their first location;
Where each side gives a part of what they like
And not stand as cobras anxious to strike.

Protester 3
Protests are not lodged in the same manner;
All are not waged with placards and banners.
Don't treat some methods with nobility
While others receive your hostility
Although I may protest differently.
Don't chastise my methods to resent me,

In essence, we should be on the same side;
Whenever justice is being denied.

Protester 4
I am not seeking personal glory;
To be interviewed to tell my story,
To be part of a group to raise a fist,
So my name can be added to the list
Of those who protest for a just cause.
Yes, I fought against unfair labor laws,
That kept us bound, suffering, but silent;
Angry, aggressive, but still nonviolent.

Protester 1
I protest to express my conviction,
Sometimes as a threat or a prediction;
But my intentions are to do no harm;
To be a prophet and sound the alarm;
To focus on the issues that matter
And on the ceilings we need to shatter;
On working conditions and wages paid;
On city streets where we are afraid.

Protester 2
I protest being taken for granted;
To level playing fields that is slanted;
The crimes perpetrated against the weak
Makes me aggressive and eager to speak
In a loud voice to show I'm not afraid
And will protest until progress is made.

I protest for I am a catalyst
For change, therefore I am an activist.

Protester 3
I protest, because we are one nation;
A country founded on demonstrations;
And therefore, won't give an apology,
When marching against inequality.
The powerless protests slow production;
But alternative forms of obstruction
Are equally expressive forms of rage;
From the same book, but a different page.

Protester 4
I protest for I am disillusioned.
The current state needs a conclusion.
I struggle with trust when folks are unfair;
When people in power won't learn to share.
And they expect the other side to bear
The burden alone when they do not care
And they in their selfishness and their greed
Will disregard others, neighbors in need.

Protester 1
I protest to release my frustrations;
To force a change in a situation;
To shift the tone of the conversation
To negligence and discrimination;
Where the unfair practices can be cited
And tensions flared and passions ignited;
And meaningful talk across a wide range

Of issues necessary to bring change.

Narrator and Protesters bow and leave the stage or stare into the camera until instructed to relax.

Fade Out:

THE END

MEANINGFUL MESSAGES

by
Orlando Ceaser

"MEANINGFUL MESSAGES"

Fade In:

Narrator

In the medical field, the medicine must get to the active site of inflammation or disease to be more effective. In combating violence, the message must be heard by anyone who is or has the capacity to perpetuate or prevent violence. We must influence all parties involved because our streets should not be the valleys of the shadow of death. Our women and children should be safe, respected and protected. The transmission and reception of positive, uplifting, constructive messages and actions can stimulate community transformation, educate our youth and protect our families. A collaborative effort is necessary to create jobs, educate our youth and return stability to families and neighborhoods. This ultimately will increase wealth and enable us to leave a positive legacy for future generations. This message applies to anyone who can make a difference to reduce violence in our society.

Reverend

If this message applies to you,
Open your heart and your eyes to
See and hear Mothers and children crying,
Innocent bystanders dying;
Neighborhoods losing their collective wealth,
An economic showing of poor health;

While bedlam and mayhem are on the loose
And citizens begging to call a truce;

If this message applies to you,
Do you think it is wise to do
Something to keep violence in check,
As whole communities become a total wreck,
As Mothers, daughters, sisters and aunts,
Want to feel safe, but realize they can't?
As wives, girlfriends and nieces;
Know that until violence ceases
They will not feel free from assaults.
The absence of safety is not their fault;
When there's a gauntlet of men at night
They brace for disrespect, fight, fright and flight.

Older Female Resident
We made progress, now we are stepping back,
As neighborhoods are under attack.
We know we have the confidence to win,
If there is no enemy from within.
We need you as part of a solution,
Not stored in a penal institution.
We need you cooperating, so we
Can leave children a positive legacy.

If this message applies to you;
You know a Mother prays and cries for you;
You're a treasured child of the Most High King;
Someone who can reduce the suffering;
Not an instrument of mass destruction,
But a mind with powers of deduction.

You have high expectations to excel
To assist families in living well.

Older Male Resident
You have talent and there is no excuse
For waging havoc and citizen abuse
On people who may be innocent souls,
As you let violence get out of control.
Life has us in a precarious plight;
As neighborhoods are subjected to blight;
A generation at risk would delight
In peaceful days and silent nights.

Bystander
You have a purpose to fulfill;
Through education and learning a skill;
Increase your chances that circumstances
Will not inhibit career advances.
By your example children will believe
That with the right effort they can achieve
The opportunities and obstacles
Will give them faith in what is possible.

Real Estate Agent
The property values will not increase
Until neighborhoods are stable and at peace.
Wealth creation is linked to real estate
We can enrich if we can educate
When residents can safely walk the streets,
Economically they will compete.

Good paying jobs are a necessity,
But land is linked to our destiny.

Church Lady
If this message applies to you,
In the name of love
This may be a surprise to you,
But we need hope.
On the streets and avenues
It is already difficult to survive,
So why make it harder to stay alive?

Nurse
If this message applies to you,
Look into the innocent eyes
Of youth born in the combat zone;
Too scared to walk the streets alone;
Having to view life as a threat;
Surprised that they are not dead yet;
Wanting desperately to be brave,
When held hostage they feel enslaved
Or living in the Wild Wild West,
Each day survival is the test.

Mail person
If this message pertains to you;
The violence and blood stains are due
To selfishly using power;
To harm the unarmed and to shower
Neighborhoods with bullet shells
And make some lives a living Hell.

If love was never shown to you
And discipline unknown to you,
We want you to know there's a better way;
Show love and lead us to a better day.

Deacon
If this violence pertains to you,
We know it is in your domain to do
Great things if you are educated.
Even though jobs have been confiscated
And balance sheets
Have side effects
And people feel the neglect
Of being treated as if rejects;
Constantly bombarded with disrespect.

Business Person
We know that,
In anger those abandoned
Don't feel the negligence is random
And broken homes and selfishness
Have left many of us with less.
But, we must work in teams,
So we can address
The problems and repair the mess
And rather than condemn,
We need redemption,
But first we must confess
And end this violent game of chess.

Reverend
If this message applies to you,
Open your heart and your eyes to
See and hear Mothers and children crying,
Innocent bystanders dying,
While bedlam and mayhem are on the loose;
And citizens begging to call a truce;
Neighborhoods losing their collective wealth,
Need to restore their economic health.

Fade Out:

THE END

MY LIFE DEFINED

by

Orlando Ceaser

"MY LIFE DEFINED"

Fade In:

Citizen 1
What does it say about my life?
In a broken world in chaos and strife;
I spend my time in shadows lurking,
Obsessed in the mundane always working
And rooted in selfishness and pleasure,
When greater issues should fill my ledger.
I spend many hours following those
Whose lives are dominated by the clothes
They wear and their exotic escapades,
Sell meaninglessness.
What a masquerade!

Citizen 2
What does it say about my life,
When I ponder who went under the knife?
Which celebrities are sleeping with whom;
Should I buy their clothing lines and perfumes;
Live vicariously, support their brands;
Enrich my status and be in demand;
To be accepted and eliminate
Good judgment as I try to imitate
Their lifestyle and their promiscuity;
Marketing flair and ingenuity,

Citizen 3
What does it say about my life
When the planet faces global warming,
I spend my time aimlessly transforming
Minor matters to make it through the day;
Glued to my devices, keeping at bay
The vital moments within each hour,
That could be used to enhance my power
But, instead of trying to be fulfilled,
Trying to be strong willed and highly skilled;
I settle for shallow, to be entertained,
When there is so much progress to be gained.

Citizen 4
What does it say about my life,
When I am immersed in stereotypes
And rehearsing scenes from my videos
And a diet of reality shows;
Synching my devices, not thinking much;
I'm staying connected, but losing touch;
While drinking the beverages advertised;
Not knowing ambition is compromised.
While homelessness is international;
I'm selfishly acting irrational.

Citizen 1
Inanimate objects become my gods.
I worship pleasure and yield to her odds.
Idols are icons on the Internet;
Life is a gamble, each day is a bet.
Bad news and sad news are around the clock;

The headlines and lyrics are aimed to shock.
In an endless array of can you top this?
Can you torment or can you drop this?
Empty and unfulfilled I am a slave
To idols and desires I crave.

Citizen 2
What does it say about my lifestyle?
If trivia rules and I seldom smile;
Voyeurism's my favorite pastime;
And I cannot remember the last time
I did something for someone other than me,
My possessions form my identity.
When I see panhandlers on the street
I turn away so our eyes won't meet.
My last significant meaningful act,
Was a long time ago when I look back.

Citizen 3
I am so obsessed with my appearance;
I want my way without interference;
Wishing I could spend time trading places,
Regretfully watching fading traces
Of dreams I abandoned along the way;
The sins of my youth were my sins to pay;
While my time was wasted in a bar;
Years later I don't know where they are.
The individuals forming my group,
Are no longer present, out of the loop.

Citizen 4
I was seeking 15 minutes of fame.
I stand on the side lines not in the game;
Addicted to pride, resistant to shame,
I wanted people to notice my name.
And so I am lost, needing to be saved
A cry for attention, for I behaved
As pleasure mongers and status seekers;
Trapped with the masses and growing weaker.

Citizen 1
What does it say about my life,
When fantasy sports and video games
Become an addiction that ruthlessly claims
The time designated for those I love
And leaves me wondering about what was
Preoccupied with my fantasy pools
And acts of rebellion by breaking rules
And living my life through college teams
Or professional sports instead of dreams.
It seems all I'm doing is marking time,
As I rush to sleep and the finished line.

Citizen 2
The economy wants knowledge workers
But I am being guided to focus on twerkers
And the contributions and interventions
Of those who shock to gain attention.
When I have a plank present in my eye,
Yet try to dismantle the other guy;
Self serving interests drive my behavior;

To take what is not mine and return the favor
And my point of view is the one's that's right;
Uniquely qualified with keen insight.

Citizen 3
In moral decay and depravity,
My soul is a gigantic cavity.
I may not excel at geography,
But I'm addicted to pornography
And pleasure shows my lack of discipline
And if I'm not careful to my chagrin,
I may encounter from my aim to please,
A sexually transmitted disease.

Citizen 4
They have marketing machines to build their brand;
Unsuspecting people don't understand
That they're sucked into a giant vortex
That will swallow time and demand more sex.
I'm lost in lust of the human body.
I break commandments with the ungodly
And the walk of shame is a constant trek
Weights on my shoulders, hands around my neck.
And I wonder if these ominous signs
Paint a picture of a life in decline.

Citizen 2
People with a dysfunctional background
Are the new role models, who will confound,
Within their unstructured philosophies
They're lost, imprisoned wanting to be free.

Their standards are weak and values vary;
And people's feelings are secondary.
There is a climate of anything goes.
I have the right to perform and who knows
What's right because everyone can be;
A self-made dysfunctional deity.

Citizen 1
Morality is apparently negotiable;
Cyber pawns we're no longer sociable
Watching self centered people who are insecure
Live through recklessness and values de jure;
Inflammatory language, vulgar speech,
Inciting emotions and words that preach
That everyone is a competitor;
Listed as either prey or predators.
And as I ponder and doubt my life,
I wonder what it says about my life.

Citizen 3
When I spend my time before the evening news
Digesting a diet of toxic views;
With a side dish of persistent gloom and doom,
I'm wondering who is sleeping with whom.
Who has a sex tape? Whose getting a divorce?
Who is in rehab, when their life is off course?
With the discretionary moments of my day;
Will I help the homeless or
Will I send them away.
Are we truly our brothers keeper?
In childhood we said losers are weepers.

Citizen 2
What does it say about my life,
When the world is on a terror watch or alert,
I am walking around with my feelings hurt,
Because someone in their uninformed state
Made a comment that I construed as hate;
When my accomplishments each day
Is moving gossip I hear others say.
I fill my life with empty calories
Of vulgar lyrics and other maladies.
I want my independence this is true,
So others can tell me what I must do.

Citizen 4
What does it say about my life,
When I pick the fruit before it is ripe,
When I could cast my net wider
To help outcasts and outsiders;
When self is at the center
I hang a sign that says
Do Not Enter;
Unless you have something
That fills a need;
Satisfies my propensity
For greed.
I know there is a purpose,
But it's not clear.
There must be a good reason,
Why I'm here.

Citizen 1
What does it say about my life
When politics becomes my religion;
And in the moment I express my zeal
I forget how to love and feel.
Obsessed with nothing but to win,
Regardless of the costs, I sin.
Civility is a rarity;
When I lash out without charity.
My actions are quietly revealing,
That my behavior is not appealing.
I need purpose, a cause to explain,
How my presence can help, so others gain.

Fade Out:

THE END

OLD PLAYER'S HOME FOR BROKEN DOWN LOVERS

by

Orlando Ceaser

"OLD PLAYER'S HOME FOR BROKEN DOWN LOVERS"

Fade In:

Setting: This fictitious account contains humor and tragedy in a home for players who live with their memoriesofpastexploits,astheyarebeyondtheirprime.

Narrator

This article, published with the writer's consent
Will tell us in detail where the old players went,
When they arrived at the end of their selfish run;
Studs put to pasture when their
playing days were done.

A residence exists on the outskirts of town;
A boarding house filled with philanderers, renown,
As sowers of wild oats with the intent to breed;
Lecherous, treacherous womanizers who's greed
Compelled these scoundrels to consistently lay claim
To their right to break hearts and never accept blame,
For they saw themselves as God's gift to womanhood;
Self proclaimed servants, who were misunderstood,
They were gifted in bed and under the covers;
These people could not love, but called
themselves lovers.

Reader 1

They were often cavalier with nothing to fear;
Smooth talkers who collected souls as souvenirs.

Their motto, "To impregnate bodies, hearts and minds
Not to leave an unsatisfied woman behind."
They would not admit to mistakes or make amends;
They always had a number of women as friends,
Few people were crafty enough to tie them down;
By using their smiles, beguiling tears of a clown;
A passionate reputation earned them their crowns;
As kings in their kingdoms and rulers in their towns.

Reader 2
Their thoughts were misguided and
focused on manhood
Which they defined as doing whatever a man could.
They walked in a room with confidence in the air,
Feeling they could claim any woman anywhere.
It was a spectacle for us to discover,
Old players in this home for broken down lovers.

Reader 1
Now they sit around tables drowning in glories,
As each one challenges the other ones stories
About some woman, somewhere who wanted to share
Their baths and their bedrooms for tender loving care.
Their tales were hyperbole mixed with allegory.
Their escapades barely scratched Earth's inventory;
The billions of women on other continents;
Beautiful women not drawn to their compliments.

Reader 2
There is not an award or a trophy given
To men who are callous and testosterone driven;

No special accommodations or accolades,
For those who caused suffering and tears to cascade.
They were living as players in the third degree
Without conscience, morality or sympathy;
Placed on this Earth, misguided they
measured their worth
By the number of women convinced to give birth.

Reader 1
Now the tired old fools sit around playing cards,
Reminiscing about when the bodies were hard,
But now between the checkers and the dominoes
And watching television with bulging egos
Set to stun, as they vaguely remember the tales
With the wind at their backs and the air in their sails
And how the young girls were foolish back in the day,
Who fell for their love service, then sent them away,
And every time the relationship had run its course,
They replaced each flower maiden without remorse.

At this stage of their game they could not recover
In the Old Players Home for Broken Down Lovers.

Reader 2
Now they sit in the Old Players home,
Under the gazebos, they sit under the dome,
Visitors are welcomed, but few will ever bring
Themselves to visit them, no siblings or offspring.
So they sit with empty expressions and blank stares,
As they're getting what they deserve for no one cares
For the broken down lovers in their special home;
For the papa's celebrated as rolling stones.

Reader 1

The Old Players Home is where lovers reminisce
About how they would tell after they had been kissed;
How soon they would register their newest conquest,
The women fell in love, but it was a contest.
This home, where dudes reflect on their
lives and their lies;
Their false confessions, notorious alibis;
They are years past their prime,
Unable to hover;
They pay for their crime
As broken down lovers;
Who collectively ruined a generation;
Through irresponsible acts of penetration.

Reader 2

The story is a fable of cause and effect;
Of injustice administered through disrespect.
The women who loved them gave them their affection;
Love and fidelity repaid with rejection;
And children of their trysts lacked financial support,
The mother's constantly dragging them to court,
While seeking karma as justice to ease the pain;
Seeking retribution through material gain;
But the years have passed and they lost the
strength to climb;
Unable to manipulate, they're short on time;
So broken down lovers have been placed on alert,
Emptiness will follow them, loneliness will hurt.

Narrator
This article, published with the writer's consent
Will tell us in detail where the old players went,
When they arrived at the end of their selfish run;
Studs put to pasture when their
playing days were done.
At this stage of their game they could not recover,
In the Old Players Home for Broken Down Lovers.

Fade Out:

THE END

THE GRASS IS THE FIRST TO GO

by
Orlando Ceaser

"THE GRASS IS THE FIRST TO GO"

Fade In:

Setting: Two residents sitting on stools talking about the plight of the neighborhood and the tell tale signs of erosion of values and real estate.

Resident 1
As poverty proliferates,
Some devalue the real estate;
Opportunity knocks but, they do not hear,
They are insecure and insincere
Their actions are timid and tentative;

Each day is a threat as they strive to live;
Trapped in neighborhoods, no means of escape;
With fewer exits they do not feel safe.

Resident 2
In addition to busting rhymes
There's the temptation to find life in crime,
They seem doubtful to grow and reach their prime
Some drop out and refuse to climb.
Fear and ignorance one day shall pass,
Apathy's evident in blades of grass.

Resident 1
We wonder whose side, gang bangers are on,
As they unwittingly become a pawn

To terror so their village streets
Are combat zones of their conceit.
They do not show love on a daily basis;
Without dreams
What the people will face is
Extinction when distinction is the key,
To a positive lasting legacy.

Resident 2
The rising crime rates that hoodlums revere
Are indications that life is severe.
The power tripping by the powerless
To terrorize neighbors already stressed.
They should know better,
Better they should know,
When tripping and slipping,
The grass is the first to go.

Resident 1
Women are afraid and disrespected,
They feel haunted, taunted and neglected.
They can't walk comfortably to exercise
Past intimidating gestures and suspicious eyes;
Property is not properly maintained,
Investors salivate for they are trained,
To watch developments and bide their time
They watch real estate prices in decline;
They cross their fingers for the markers show,
That the grass is the first to go.

Resident 2
The silent creep of gentrification
Will sweep through quickly and its penetration
Will oversee the disintegration
Of neighborhoods identification;
Since they are sitting on prime real estate;
Cultivate their homes and gain a good rate;
Meticulously care and maintain their lawns;
To influence how school districts are drawn.

Resident 1
Neighborhood watch, curfews and civic pride;
Everyone out in the open with nothing to hide;
Hard work, excellence and etiquette
With education as the key to get
Net worth,
To rise as it changes the market,
Revenue and cash flow,
Have a new target.

Resident 2
When streets are crime infested,
Family fortunes are lost.
They lose most of the money invested
And they cannot recoup the cost.
Devalued property
And lost revenue,
Prevent banks from coming
To the rescue.

Resident 1
We stare through windows and peer through the glass.
We see the problems that go beyond class,
The indicators, early warning signs
Affect sleep as upkeep is out of line;
The symptoms that people should recognize;
Deteriorating before their eyes;
The increase in vacant lots tend to show,
Progress is slow,
But the grass is the first to go.

Fade Out:

THE END

THE PRISONER'S PLEDGE

by

Orlando Ceaser

"THE PRISONER'S PLEDGE"

Fade In:

Voice 1
I am greater than a perpetrator.

Voice 2
My confinement is not my assignment.

Voice 3
My sentence led to my repentance.

Voice 4
I can advance beyond my circumstance
And make the most of a second chance.

Voice 1
To the outside world I have vanished;
Exiled from relatives and my peers;
As a prisoner I was banished;
But, destined to rise despite their fears.

Voice 2
My image may be soiled and tarnished,
And though I have issues to address;
As wood to be sanded and varnished;
My rough edges won't suppress success.

Voice 3
I will take time and use it wisely;
Allow each moment to advise me.

I will find glory within my story;
To reach the purpose I must fulfill;
Through education and learn a skill.

Voice 4
I will man up and shoulder the load;
And spare my enemies of my wrath;
Discouraging others from this road
And pledge to place them on the right path.

Voice 1
To reach a purpose in my life;

Voice 2
Not decided by a gun or knife;

Voice 3
Weapons, by force or character flaws;

Voice 4
Actions that are deemed against the laws.

All
I pledge to make a difference now;
And if profiled, in a way typecast;
This covenant is my solemn vow,
To not repeat the sins of the past.

Fade Out:

THE END

THE GRASS IS THE FIRST TO GO: DISCUSSION GUIDE

WE CAN MAXIMIZE the value of our time if we see it as an investment. We can begin with entertainment. We all like to be entertained, but can we take it to another level? Can we also be educated by these engagements? Can we move on to be inspired to a positive action from these encounters? If we are educated and inspired by our entertainment, this will then enable us to increase the value we receive from the time we spend on various experiences. Our perspectives will be broadened, and we will increase our understanding and connections with others, as we gain a greater appreciation of how and why others think and feel the way they do.

It is a good practice to have movie screening parties, followed by a structured debate. This technique is related to the agenda in book clubs where the members analyze and apply the intricacies of a good book.

Our impressions of people are shaped by many factors. Racial, ethnic and cultural messages are implanted in us at various stages of our lives. This natural conditioning from family, friends and others who are just like us, subconsciously shapes our views. Communication vehicles such as the various types of news reporting and advertising shape our thinking and perceptions. We are influenced by how individuals and groups are portrayed in the various venues where we receive information. They place into our awareness the items and issues they think we should find important.

When you experience The Grass is the First to Go, apply the mindset of entertainment, education and inspiration toward a positive action. You may absorb the messages line by line or thought by thought, for the speakers have something provocative to say.

This Discussion guide is set up to supplement your thoughts and feelings after experiencing the one-act plays. The recommendations for discussion are not meant to be all inclusive. The reader is free to explore a myriad of perspectives. Treat these guidelines as a catalyst for provocative conversations that will ultimately lead to individual action plans, promises and commitments that spring from a better understanding of the issues presented.

You may not have the time and do not feel required to address all of the questions and recommendations. Circle those that seem interesting and write your own recommendations for greater personalization and relevance.

A STRANGER: THE LEGEND OF A RANDOM BLACK GUY

THE MOTIVATION BEHIND this piece originates in individuals we consider as the other or the stranger in our lives. They are unknown to us and, therefore, suspicious. We attach fear and negative images to them. You may discuss the negative thoughts you harbor toward others and discuss the headlines, news and other stories that play into your impressions.

Whereas the focus is on the random Black Guy, I could have just as easily inserted any race, culture or ethnicity. You could interchange any difference or distinction you may want to highlight. You could have a discussion around the question "Am I attractive enough? smart enough, rich enough, or popular enough?" There may be instances where someone wants you to feel inadequate or deficient in order to bring you down to earth in their eyes.

Bias and stereotypes may explain some of the exclusionary behavior others direct your way. You may define and discuss these practices during your small group, book club or classroom conversations. The following questions may also help guide your time together.

1. Why do we negatively profile individuals or groups?

2. What must we do as a society or as individuals to eliminate the practices of negative profiling?
3. Define unconscious bias, preferences and stereotypes and discuss these definitions with the group.
4. Discuss the motive behind different perspectives and eyewitness testimonies. Two individuals could look at the same event and come away with vastly different interpretations. How is this possible and why does it happen?
5. How do we relate to someone who holds a different point of view?
6. How did we arrive at our ethnic, cultural and racial understanding of people?
7. Review and discuss comments regarding the way people are treated in social settings, while shopping or interacting with others.
8. How do you respond to these stories? Do you believe them? Why?
9. The images we develop in the United States are often exported to other countries. Are you aware of the impressions others outside of the United States may have of African-Americans based on the information we have shared overseas? Movies studios and promoters have suggested that movies with an African-American in the lead role do not sell as well in many markets outside of the United States. Consider

how the media or other factors may contributed to that phenomenon.

10. How do we invite others into our world and make them feel comfortable? I am reminded of comments made about a particular racial or ethnic group always sitting together in school settings, or self-segregating in a sense. Are similar comments made when, for example, all of the members of the cheerleading squad or debate team sit together. It is quite common for among other "groups" to sit together without similar comments of suspicion being made. How do we address these comments or situations?

AFFIRMATIONS IN INCARCERATION

AFFIRMATIONS IN INCARCERATION were written to project positive thoughts on those who are in prison or have served time behind bars. They are also designed for those who may role-play or listen to these scenarios for educational purposes. These affirmations may be challenged or validated by those who have been incarcerated for their authenticity and relevance. They are written in the first person, but may also be received in the third person.

1. Which of these comments pertain to me and how have they influenced my story?
2. How have I continued the same legacy?
3. What can I do to make a difference in my life?
4. How will I ensure that I will not make the same mistakes again?
5. How will I be a mentor to keep others from following my same path?
6. How can I give myself permission to change?
7. Who can I stay strong and committed to change?
8. Do I believe that I can change?
9. Do I believe that I can make a difference in the lives of others?
10. How can my faith convince me and others that God is not finished with me yet?

ALIEN NATE AND ME

A BEST FRIEND is someone you can talk to, relate to and feel comfortable with. A best friend is always a plus in making life more interesting and enjoyable. The influence of this individual extends to the workplace. Individuals who have a best friend at work are more likely to be fully engaged in their work activities and will have a more positive view of work.

We have heard of children and even some adults who had an imaginary friend. This friend, whether an animal or human, served as a confidante, someone they could speak to and share their stories and thoughts. Many of us appreciate having someone we can talk to, whether real or imaginary. James Stewart, in the classic movie Harvey, had such a friend. Harvey was an invisible rabbit.

I often feel that we need an objective person to evaluate the circumstances that engulf the human race. I feel it would be intriguing to have someone observe our condition and ask valid questions, as a third-party observer. They could challenge us and hold us accountable. Alien Nate and Me serve that purpose.

1. Read each paragraph and give your comments about the questions asked by Nate and the response given by Me.
2. List the major issues brought up by Nate in the conversation.

3. What do you think we should do about the various issues surfaced?
4. What role can you play to make a difference in some of these areas?
5. What are we doing to develop values and morality in ourselves and others?
6. What can we do personally to make this world a better place?
7. What are you doing to change your environment?
8. What can we do to ensure people receive a moral foundation?
9. How can we use our influence to hold ourselves and others accountable for our actions?

AM I BLACK ENOUGH?

MANY AFRICAN-AMERICANS have stories to tell about their experiences with the question, "Am I Black enough?" They could go into great depths explaining each encounter, the insecurity generated and what they did to prove the person wrong who challenged their "Blackness." If they did not have a similar experience to someone from their neighborhood, they were somehow made to feel unqualified to be Black. I attended a youth panel where one of the participants discussed challenges being accepted by her peers at a new high school because she spoke differently, had different interests and was brought up in a different neighborhood (a predominantly white area). There is a tendency among some African-Americans to assimilate within their own community. Some members of the community establish a certain mindset from their experience and expect everyone else to follow along. If you fall outside of that mindset or modus operandi, you may be subject to ridicule and derision by those who believe everyone should fit within a prescribed mold.

Diversity and inclusion is therefore important within and across all communities. "Am I Black enough?" is a question that can provide a forum for rich discussion about the power of difference which will enable us to take advantage of our talents, skills, abilities and perspectives.

1. Discuss the motivation behind why someone's authenticity is being questioned. You may

discuss assimilation, the concept of being uppity, bourgeoisie or an Uncle Tom. Are some people perceived as the standard for "Blackness?" Why does someone feel the need to knock someone off their high horse, bring them down to earth or put them in their place?

2. If you have personal experience with the question, tell the group or reflect on how you handled it? For example, you may have responded "I am not speaking white, I am speaking right."
3. Have you seen young people change their speech and behavior to fit it?
4. How do you counsel young people who are changing their behavior to be accepted by others?
5. What do you say to youth who struggle with the same situation?
6. Provide examples and personal stories about someone who changed to be tough enough, brave enough or relevant enough.
7. Give examples of those who faced the same dilemma, but maintained who they were and did not change.
8. Discuss positive and negative peer pressure regarding the detriment and benefits.
9. What can we do to protect those who wish to stand their ground and abide by their values and principles?

10. What can we do to strengthen others to resist conforming to activities that are detrimental to their development?
11. Discuss the legacy of excellence among the Kings and Queens and people of high standing in history, in the family and the community, past and present.

I PROTEST

1. Discuss the reasons people protest, keeping in mind a historical perspective.
2. Discuss the right to protest and the counter protest.
3. List some current and historical protest movements.
4. Discussing historical issues and debate whether the goals would have been achieved without formal protest (women's voting rights, fair wages and benefits, sexual harassment, civil rights, LGBTQ rights and political positions, etc.)
5. Discuss protest in relationship to sharing power.
6. How do you feel when traffic is backed up or you are otherwise inconvenienced as a result of a protest?
7. Do you try to understand the different sides of an issue when people protest?
8. What are your thoughts about an individual's right to protest?
9. How do you register your support for a particular issue?
10. Do you take up your civic obligation to participate in the democratic process of making your voice heard?

11. What are your comments about Black Lives Matter and other movements that involve civil disobedience?
12. How can we serve as peace makers for those who wish to state their views?
13. What ways do you use to show support for or speak out against injustice or a cause close to your heart?
14. What can you do to ensure that protests are peaceful and productive?
15. Do you believe protests have to be peaceful?

MEANINGFUL MESSAGES

HOW OFTEN HAVE you thought that the people who are most in need of change frequently do not hear or receive the messages that would help them? We have strong feelings about what must be done in a particular situation. We strongly feel that the people involved must change in some manner. We state powerfully what should be done, but the people responsible for the turmoil is not present or a part of the solution-generating process.

This same process happens a lot with violence in communities. Most would agree that jobs must be provided to impact the level of violence some of our communities. At the same time, we also agree that there is still a need for respect of authority, women, the elderly and children. Violence is a complicated issue that must be addressed on many different levels. However, the people causing the violence must have a seat at the table. They may not be in the meeting, see the program against their actions or attend the marches demanding them to stop the violence.

1. How do we ensure that people respect and protect our elders, women and children?
2. What must we do as a society or as an individual to eliminate these practices?
3. How do we ensure that we have all available parties at the table on major issues?

4. What can we do to bring jobs into the community?
5. What can we do to ensure that money and jobs stay in the community?
6. What can we do to build entrepreneurship in our youth?
7. How can we give our youth hope and something to strive for?
8. How can we give youth a strong educational foundation to increase their options?
9. What can we do to expand their exposure to the world around them?
10. Does being poor automatically make you prone to violent behavior?
11. How does poverty affect morality?
12. How do we instill values in our youth?
13. What are the key values you want your children to see and practice?
14. Who is currently responsible for building character and values into our youth?
15. How often do you as a family, have regularly scheduled meals and activities to bond with each other?

MY LIFE DEFINED

OUR PRIORITIES SEEM out of place. We spend time, effort and money focused on matters that are trivial in the grand scheme of things. There are natural and unnatural disasters and calamities that find people at war, experiencing violence and poverty. There are racial, cultural and ethnic tensions and genocide, as man continues to mistreat fellow members of the human race. We are immersed in selfishness and pleasure seeking, and have accumulated numerous ways of escapism purely for gratification and living in the moment. We must ask ourselves what can we do to add value and meaning to our lives?

1. What are we doing to benefit others?
2. Do we volunteer in areas where the focus is on easing the suffering of someone else?
3. What are we doing to develop ourselves mentally, physically, spiritually and emotionally?
4. Is spiritual growth and belief in God a part of our mindset and lifestyle?
5. How do you define success for you personally?
6. Do you have a plan and what are the elements of your plan?
7. Discuss good deeds performed where you did not personally benefit (your goal was to help someone and not receive personal praise and recognition).

8. Why are we attracted to certain people, programs and issues?
9. Discuss the key areas mentioned in the play for reflection and discussion.
10. What are our practices and timetable for reviewing the consistency between our beliefs and our actions?

OLD PLAYERS HOME FOR BROKEN DOWN LOVERS

WE HAVE GLAMORIZED men in our culture by giving them the label of "player." Individuals who are free, unattached and uncommitted are idolized by men young and old. There's an element of being cool that comes with the moniker of player. Men who spend their lives shirking responsibility and commitment have fathered children out of wedlock and have worn the title, as a badge of honor. We call their women "Baby Mammas" and many times these players are irresponsible in caring for their children. Often times they were not there for the rearing of their children, but they were cool.

All players are not irresponsible individuals. With many, it was just a way of saying that being a player meant that they were popular and in demand. However, the focus of the Old Players Home for Broken down Lovers is around the consequences of players who are the irresponsible type. They have a disruptive impact on the fabric of the family. Additionally, they may be contributors to the disrespect that men have toward the women. These old players were role models for younger men and women and perpetuated the notion of selfishness and self-gratification, and received their just desserts. They may have harassed and disrespected women and exerted power over them.

1. What are we doing today to perpetuate the idea that being a player is a desirable personality type?
2. How are we training young men and women to respect each other?
3. Are we training young boys and girls around abstinence and taking pride in their bodies?
4. What are we doing to ensure that women are not seen and treated as sex objects?
5. What can we do to ensure women and men are not sexually harassed?
6. What can we do to be aware that people's rights are being violated?
7. What are we doing to train our young men and women about discipline and delaying gratification?
8. What can we do to ensure that young men and women are safe and protected from predators?
9. Discuss situations where absentee parents had a negative effect on the upbringing of their children.
10. What can we do to volunteer our services to help young men and women pursue their dreams?
11. How are we training our youth to honor and respect their elders?
12. Discuss the circumstances of the old players and what led them to their current predicament?

13. Discuss their lifestyle choices and how it affected them and their relationships.
14. Can you identify with the players and how you have been influenced by similar behavior?
15. How has the publicity around sexual harassment and the #MeToo campaign affected your thinking and actions?

THE GRASS IS THE FIRST TO GO

MANY TIMES, OUR exterior is a reflection of the interior. We know that we can't always judge a book by its cover. Because, many of us may look good on the outside, but are miserable and disorganized on the inside. It is important to have discipline in many areas of our lives. As we take the time to cultivate our appearance, which is our outside, we should also look for ways to ensure that our values on the inside, our content are an accurate reflection of who we want to be. There are instances when someone is having difficulty with a transition into a neighborhood or other situations. We need to help in these transitions by making people feel comfortable and not judging them and setting up a self-fulfilling prophecy with a negative outcome.

1. What are we doing to ensure that we have our act together on the inside and the outside?
2. What are we doing to ensure that we are paying attention to detail in the important areas of our lives, such as relationships, finances and career?
3. How are we maintaining our focus on education and on our careers?
4. How are we holding ourselves accountable for the things that matter most to us?
5. How are we emphasizing a moral foundation based on values?

6. Are we taking advantage of financial literacy courses?
7. Are we ensuring that our children understand the value of managing their money?
8. What are we doing to ensure that our children are disciplined by having structure and giving them responsibilities, i.e. chores, boundaries, etc.?
9. Are you giving children guidance in making decisions?
10. Are we paying attention to our children's friends and their influence over their actions?
11. Are we treating elders, women and children with dignity and respect?
12. Are we active in our communities to ensure that we are enhancing our property values?
13. Are we taking care of our property?
14. Are we taking care of our bodies and our minds?
15. Are we spending time with our children, scheduling meals together and engaging in conversations over dinner and listening to their concerns?
16. What are we doing to reach out to others to ensure they have a smooth transition into the community?

THE PRISONER'S PLEDGE

PLEDGES ARE DECLARATIONS that we make to ourselves and others to show our intentions. The Prisoners Pledge contains positive messages that have a universal application.

1. Discuss the pledge and the key messages.
2. Can we create similar personal pledges prior to committing offenses?
3. How do you hold yourself accountable to deliver the pledges, affirmations and positive routines?

ABOUT THE AUTHOR — ORLANDO CEASER

ORLANDO CEASER IS a writer, professional speaker, thought leader and voiceover specialist for Watchwell Communications, Inc., OrlandoCeasercom. He spent his first career as a business executive in the pharmaceutical industry. He has over 30 years of experience in sales, management, training, diversity, marketing, leadership and personal development. He aspires to entertain, educate and inspire people to unlock their leadership greatness to reach their dreams.

Mr. Ceaser advises students and employees to become Impact Players in school, work and in their communities. Impact players are individuals who are prominent and dominant in their fields. They are the game changes who improve performance through their actions. Impact Players are difference makers who positively influence individual and team performance. Mr. Ceaser has presented to prisoners and those responsible for ministering to them. He presents two decision making models; The Know System™ and The Objection Model – The Art of Refusal™. These models guide users to make decisions consistent with their faith and value systems. Mr. Ceaser is the author of eleven books including Unlock your Leadership Greatness, Leadership above the Rim, The Isle of Knowledge, Look for the Blessing and Leadership Greatness through High Performance Poetry. His blog, The "O" Zone (myozonelayer.com) focuses on management, motivation and leadership.

Mr. Ceaser has three spoken word CD's, *Teach the Children to Dance, Leadership Collection* and *My Queen*. He also has developed two comic strips, *Cocky & Rhodette* and *Cocky Jr.,* candidly and humorously address life in the corporate world and the teenage years, respectively. Mr. Ceaser also served on the drama team at Willow Creek Community Church in South Barrington, IL and performed voiceover projects for both Willow Creek and Lakewood Church in Houston, Texas.

Mr. Ceaser and his wife reside in South Barrington, Illinois.

I received a lot of wisdom from from my father, Norrell Ceaser, Sr. WISDOM for me will always stand for "What I Should Demand Of Myself."